AFGHANISTAN
1970-1975

Images From an Era of Peace

Photographs by Joseph Hoyt

"The photos ... are a valuable record of this era. By exposing them to a wider audience we may hope to encourage viewers to better understand the lives of the Afghan people and further the cause of rebuilding Afghanistan after so many years of war and turbulence. These photos show the nation poised to embrace the future. People and places, daily life and individual livelihoods are shown in a positive light. Mr. Hoyt has sought to reveal the real Afghanistan of the former era."

Hamed Elmi
Cultural Attaché, Embassy of Afghanistan
Washington, DC

"My reaction to the images is that the world should see Afghanistan as it was before all the wars rolled across that nation, with the hope in our hearts that Afghanistan can be at peace again ..."

"...it is my hope that others can see the images as I saw them and realize Afghanistan is not a remote and distant place filled with incomprehensible people, but a land filled with people who love, laugh and raise children just as we do."

Clyde Butcher
Fine arts photographer and environmentalist
www.clydebutcher.com

(this was) ... "a time when Afghanistan was peaceful and still little known in the West, the images depict a country prior to the deluge. There are hints of what's to come, but mostly one is left with powerful feelings of nostalgia and remorse."

"Mr. Hoyt's work is thus reminiscent of August Sander's great Westpahlen portraits made between World Wars I and II. It is important that we be reminded of what was lost during the two decades of unrelenting war and revolution in Afghanistan. Mr. Hoyt's work does exactly that, and I recommend it with enthusiasm."

Michael L. Carlebach
Professor Emeritus, University of Miami
Coral Gables, FL

"The most beautiful example is the scene of the market in Feyzabad. It is astonishing by the importance of the vegetation, the presence in harmony of various Afghan ethnic groups living according to traditions now forgotten because of years of war and dryness."

"Being myself Afghan, I am grateful toward Mr. Hoyt to emphasize the culture and the history of this much ignored country."

Mr. Zaia Khalid
Editor of the project Afghanistan Old Photographs
Limoges, FRANCE
www.afghanistan-photos.com

Dear Readers:

The first time I spoke to Khaled Hosseini at his home in San Francisco, I thanked him for changing the images in my head. I called him in preparation for presenting our distinguished *Literature to Life Award* to him in Spring 2005. After reading his book, *The Kite Runner*, I no longer thought of bombings and caves and terrorists when I thought of Afghanistan. Instead, my imagery had expanded to include children smiling, marketplaces filled with activity and wondrous ancient landscapes awakening at dawn.

What magnificent fortune to now have those images come to life through the artistry of Joseph Hoyt. Joe's photographs adorn the wall of my office at the American Place Theatre In New York City, looking out toward the mighty Hudson River. They speak of the strength and character of a people who embrace their heritage and celebrate their homeland.

As the Theatre presents our performances of *The Kite Runner* in schools and communities across America, we have direct impact on teachers' and students' lives. One of the initial and most crucial steps towards a deep educational experience is sending out our Resource Guides to introduce the world of the book to that audience. The photographs you are about to see are the soul of that material and help us engage in a personal dialogue that transcends words and moves us toward that place that only quality visual art can. They speak of the past and the future and of hope and of a life worth living.

I am humbled and proud to have Joe's artistry as a vital part of the work we do to bring stories and literature to life.

Sincerely,

David Kener
Executive Director

The American Place Theatre
New York, NY 10018

AFGHANISTAN 1970-1975
Images From an Era of Peace

The photographs in this collection reveal an Afghanistan very different from the one we know today. What we see in these images is not just an Afghanistan at peace, but also a people at peace with themselves, going about their daily routines.

Taken over thirty years ago and unseen by the public until 2005, the photographs show the vibrancy and nuance of an ancient culture nearly lost to 25 years of war and political turmoil. They portray the laughing children and the handsome faces of a rugged and courageous people living as they have for centuries. These images were taken prior to the Russian invasion and many years before civil war wracked the country and allowed the establishment of the murderous rule of the Taliban and invasion of foreign fighters.

From the perspective of a young traveler one might say the 1970s saw Afghanistan at its best. With only recently opened borders, the country offered a kind of adventure travel not often seen since: safe, inexpensive travel through a land of towering mountains concealing verdant orchards and untouched torrents, vast deserts, wandering nomad tribes, and a welcoming people generous far beyond their means.

These images show a wide breadth of the country from intimate portraits to the towering 5th-century Buddhas of Bamian, since destroyed by Taliban extremists. The photographs convey a complex Afghanistan, a culture rich in history and tradition but modernizing and connecting to the outside world. The exhibition includes candid shots of Afghans at work and at play. Taken at a time when political content would have been irrelevant, when seen as a whole the exhibition offers the viewer a refreshing change from the ubiquitous, dreary media images of Afghanistan today.

This was a time when the economy was thriving, people were working and there was a burgeoning tourist trade. Libraries, schools and universities were open to most. Food was plentiful. Gardens and orchards were lovingly tended, and the ancient irrigation systems functioned as they had for centuries. The most beautiful fruits and vegetables in all of Central Asia could be had in the local markets. The bazaars were brimming with antique carpets, jewelry, beadwork and textiles. Foreign aid had built fine highways and the modern airports at Kabul and Kandahar were served by airlines from Europe, Russia, India and beyond.

The Afghans loved their King, Mohammed Zahir Shah. They prayed, and they loved their land, their gardens and their families. Afghanistan was then a nation with a thriving intellectual community with free exchange of ideas, respectful of its rich cultural heritage and seemingly willing to embrace its ethnic diversity. Hidden from the casual traveler, however, were political, religious and cultural factors that would, in the ensuing years, radically change the Afghanistan I was experiencing.

To be sure, this was a poor country; then, as now, one of the poorest on the planet. But this was a nation hidden away in central Asia with a recorded history dating to before 3000 BC. The ancient land had seen the coming of Alexander the Great and was an outpost of Greek culture. In the 3rd - 5th centuries it had been a great center of Buddhist culture and learning. It was the home of Tamerlane and had been invaded by Genghis Khan. The city of Balkh, known since antiquity as the Mother of Cities, located near present day Mazar-i-Sharif, was the birthplace of the beloved Sufi poet Jellaludin Rumi.

The Afghanistan we know today is a nation laid waste by more than 25 years of war and discord. Ten years of Russian occupation have left the land littered with perhaps millions of land mines. Many thousands of Afghans have been killed and countless others have been maimed, blinded, displaced and nearly forgotten. This and the brutal rule of the Taliban, even now in resurgence, have changed the country and its people, perhaps forever. Hope for Afghanistan's future may lie in our ability to look back at an era in its recent past when the nation was at peace.

My hope is that the viewer will experience a bit of the dignity, humanity, good will and humor that I found in these wonderful people and enjoy a glimpse of their fabled and beautiful land. The images show the spirit and resilience of a nearly lost culture. I want the viewer to see that the Afghan people deserve support as they try to rebuild their nation. Regional and world peace and security require this. But more importantly, the love and respect of all mankind require it of of us all.

Joseph Hoyt
2008

DEDICATION

In memory of Barry M. Bransfield.
It was in the darkroom in his Boston apartment
that these images first came to life in 1971.

He would be pleased to see they have been resurrected.

AFGHANISTAN
1970-1975

Images From an Era of Peace

AKS MISTAR?
KABUL, 1973
This gesture, hands to the eyes, accompanied by the question *Aks Mistar?* (Photo Mister?) is often heard while walking around with a camera around one's neck. A bird seller, or *kowk froosh,* sits near his stall on Kabul's famed Chicken Street, known as *Koch-i-Murga* to local shoppers. Several styles of birdcages, or *qafas,* are seen; those for fighting birds (*powdahah*) and singing birds (*jal*).

NINETEEN BOYS
KABUL, 1973
Young men crowd the back street shop of a teacher, or *moalem,* to laugh and study verses from the Holy Koran. The legend on the booklet held by the boys reads *Sephakha Alam de Lala* and translates as Verse Alam de Lala. The boys were eager to be photographed and the teacher, who is just off camera, was pleased to oblige.

BATCHA
JALALABAD, 1971
The common reference for a young boy is
batcha. This child is dressed in typical
attire: a skullcap, vest and around his
neck a talisman, or *tahweez*, containing
written prayers.

FOUR UZBEK SHEEPHERDERS
BADAKHSHAN PROVINCE, 1971
These young men, wearing typical
long robes, or *chapans,* tend their
flock near their home. The entrance
to their compound is seen in the
background: a tall mud and rock wall
with a wooden entry door.

BIRDCAGES
KANDAHAR, 1973
Bird sellers, or *kowk froosh,* relax while waiting for prospective customers. They sell birds trained for fighting and small songbirds treasured for their musical calls. They may be seen carrying a small kettle, or *chai-josh,* for the cup of tea taken often during the day regardless of the season.

TWO POLICEMEN ENCOUNTERED ON THE STREET IN JALALABAD, 1971

BLACKSMITH
KABUL, 1973
A sidewalk blacksmith, or *aahangar,* puts the finishing touches on a set of horseshoes, or *naal-asp.*

AFGHANISTAN 1970-1975
Images From an Era of Peace
Photographs by Joseph Hoyt

For years now, Afghanistan has become synonymous with the Taliban, Al-Qaeda and terrorism. But it wasn't always so. For most of the previous century, Afghanistan lived in peaceful anonymity. It was a magnet for travelers who came to see the rugged beauty of the land, to walk along the old Silk Route and to meet its kind and hospitable people. Joseph Hoyt's lens gloriously brings back this bygone Afghanistan. In his photos we get a glimpse of a land that once was a meeting point of cultures, a link between east and west. He captures the raw beauty of this land, a taste of its prosperous history and the unique spirit of its proud and resilient people. What's more, looking at Hoyt's photographs of this happier era, the suffering and tumult that the Afghan people have endured since is made more personal. The toll of the tragedy becomes palpable. This is a testament to Hoyt's skill as a photographer as well as his personal affection for this war-scarred land and its people.

Khaled Hosseini
Author of two best-selling novels of Afghanistan - <u>The Kite Runner</u> and <u>A Thousand Splendid Suns</u>

AFGHANISTAN 1970-1975
Images From an Era of Peace
Photographs by Joseph Hoyt

The 64 page exhibition catalogue with 50 high quality duotone images and photographer's comments is available for $20.00 plus s&h.
Visit the website **www.imagesofafghanistan.com** for complete details.
Contact Joseph Hoyt at **imagesofafghanistan@gmail.com**
Payment accepted through PayPal or by personal check.
Shipments made worldwide.

The museum exhibition of the entire collection of 50 images and artifacts is available through **www.artvisionexhibtions.com**.
Contact Victoria Ann Rehberg at 561-883-2145.
Email: **vrehberg@artvisionexhibitions.com**

SINABAND FROOSH
KABUL, 1974
The proprietor of a makeshift brassiere shop responds to the photographer's amusement at his inventory of oversized undergarments, known as *sinaband*.

BUS TOP
ON THE ROAD NEAR CHARIKAR, 1974
Sitting on the top of a bus is the preferred way to see the countryside; it is cool, uncrowded and usually provides dust-free passage to one's destination.   Bus lines, or *serwes*, provide access to most places in Afghanistan at nominal cost.

BUS WINDOW
KABUL, 1973
An elderly passenger leans from
the window of a bus as it leaves a
terminal in Kabul.

CAMEL DRIVER
KABUL, 1973
A Pashtoon tribesman rests with his camels at a Kabul livestock market. His turban, or *lungi*, composed of some seven meters of narrow cloth, and waistcoat, or *waskat*, are common attire for many Afghan men.

CARRYING A LOAD OF FODDER
NEAR JALALABAD, 1971
The man facing the camera carries a load
of animal fodder wrapped in a large piece
of cloth. As he rests on a wall, chatting
with an acquaintance, the mountains of
Nuristan can be seen in the distance.

ENTRANCE TO A *CHAI KHANA*
FEYDZBAD, 1971
The proprietor greets guests at the door of a teahouse, sometimes called a *hotal.* In the left corner, a wood-fired oven, or *bukhari,* heats water for tea. The minstrel at the right holds a crudely made two stringed *dambour*.

SIDEWALK COBBLER
KABUL, 1971
The open-air shop of a shoe repairman, or *buut-rangi,* features a variety of laces, polishes and repair materials, including an automobile tire inner tube.

THE BABAIE WALE HOTEL
KANDAHAR, 1970
The sign above this hotel at
the center of Kandahar near
the Herat Gate reads
Maineger Abdul Sammd
promising *Happeniss Claen
Badrowm, showar chep for
torest*. This was a favorite
stopover for frugal travelers.

A VIEW DOWN A DUSTY KABUL BACKSTREET, 1974
Modernist architecture and contemporary power poles on the left and an ancient mud brick wall on the right juxtapose different moments in time.

HAULING FREIGHT
KABUL, 1971
Two young Hazara men maneuver an unimaginable load through Kabul bazaar. The two-wheeled cart, known as a *karachy,* is typically fitted with a recycled truck axle and tires.

WOODSELLER
WINTER, KABUL, 1971
A wood-seller, or *chob-froosh,* stands in front of his supply of split walnut. The triangular arrangement on the left is a scale. Measures of weight he might employ would be yak *pow, char ak, and yak seer* - one pound, four pounds and sixteen pounds respectively.

ASLEEP ON A *CHARPAAY*
KANDAHAR, 1973
A man naps on a typical rope strung bed, or *charpaay* - literally meaning four feet.   Beds such as these are often fitted with thick, futon-like mattresses, but it is not uncommon for one to sleep on the bare *respan munjee,* or jute rope.

A CLOSE SHAVE WITH A DULL RAZOR
KABUL, 1971
The client grimaces as a barber, or *dalak,*
uses an old-fashioned straight razor to
put the finishing touches on a sidewalk
haircut. Sidewalk vendors of all kinds
may be seen throughout the country.

VILLAGE FOOTPATH
BAMIAN, 1970
A view down a garden path, or
kucha-baghi, framed by an ancient
adobe wall on one side and a stand
of poplars on the other, reveals a
glimpse of the great Buddha.

THE GREAT BUDDHA
BAMIAN, 1970
Two huge Buddhas carved into the sandstone cliffs at Bamian are Afghanistan's most recognized archeological symbols. Created in the 3rd - 5th centuries A.D. and standing some 175 feet tall, the larger of the statues dominated this lovely valley for nearly 1500 years before being destroyed by Taliban extremists who saw them as idolatrous symbols contrary to the tenets of Islam.

DECORATIONS ON A HOLY MAN'S TOMB
NEAR GHAZNI, 1973
This type of decorated tomb, or *ziarat,* features two metallic hands representing the hands of Ali, son-in-law of the Prophet Mohammed. Each hand bears the inscription *Allah.* The fabric strips are often made of green cloth, the holiest color, and also white cloth, which symbolizes peace. It has been stated that the display of flags in such a case may have its origin in the Buddhist practice of placing multi-colored flags on tombs and shrines.

KABUL RIVER THOROUGHFARE
KABUL, 1975
A narrow bank of the Kabul River has become a pedestrian walkway. In the background is a mosque and a minaret from which the *muezzin* will make the *adhan,* or call to Friday prayer, and the five-times daily call to prayer, *salat*.

GRAIN MERCHANT
FEYDZABAD, 1971
Neat cones of rice are offered for sale in a market stall in Feyzabad located in the far northeast of the country. The metal pan and components of a scale are seen nearby.

BADAKHSHAN MARKET TREE
FEYDZABAD, 1971
A massive ancient shade tree, perhaps a *chinar*, or Asian sycamore, dominates the village bazaar. Badakhshan Province extends into the Wakhan Corridor, the narrow sliver of land where Afghanistan has a short border with China. A variety of dried fruits and nuts are offered for sale as are the oft-seen birdcages.

A HORSE, A MAN AND A CARRIAGE TOP
KANDAHAR, 1973
A horse wiles away his time near a shade-house type of structure called a *chapary*, made of woven grass or reeds. A man sits nearby shielding his face from the sun. In the back left resides a collection of water jugs and bowls.

STEPPING STONES
NEAR KABUL, 1973
Strategically placed stones offer two men dry footed passage across a shallow tributary of the Kabul River.

THE VILLAGE OF LASH-I-JOUAYN, 1971
Deep in the southwest desert, near the Iranian border and the fabled ruins of Chakhansur and where the Helmand River seems to disintegrate into marshes and seasonal lakes, this ancient town presents itself near sunset as a vision from another age. The distinctive domed architecture and construction, known as *jumbazee*, is reminiscent of desert architecture the world over. Constructed without wood, the mud brick homes provide welcome reprieve from the desert heat.

A VIEW INTO A PRIVATE COMPOUND
KANDAHAR, 1973
A birds-eye view into the inner courtyard allows one to view an Afghan family in their private home. Notable are the vaulted roofs of the various houses and the drying clothes. Beyond the walls hand dug channels carry fresh water to the fields, which are criss-crossed with narrow paths for access to the crops.

KANDAHAR LANDSCAPE WITH *QALA*, 1973
Mud walls demarcate property lines while in the background fortress-like walls of a fort, or *qala*, surround a private home.

NOMAD TRADERS IN THE KHYBER PASS, 1971
Two traders with their heavily laden camels on their way through the fabled Khyber Pass into Pakistan.

KIDS BUS RIDE
KABUL, 1974
It is commonplace to see youngsters riding the bus alone. Here, two young boys, bundled against the cold, hold on tight as they leave a Kabul bus stop.

NEIGHBORHOOD KIDS CHASING A PHOTOGRAPHER, 1971
Running backward, the photographer encourages this joyous crowd as they shout *aks mistar* and *Mistar Catchalou* - or Mr. Potato.
Probably no foreigner ever walked down a Kabul street without being called Mistar Catchalou, the meaning of which is open to interpretation.

LIZARDS AS MEDICINE
KABUL, 1974
On the Jada-i-Maiwand, a major shopping street, a child tends to a strange collection in a sidewalk display. Several live lizards, forelegs tied together with thread, and numerous unidentified medicine bottles to treat some mysterious ailments await a prospective buyer.

READING ON CHICKEN STREET
KABUL, 1973

VILLAGE POTTER
BAMIAN, 1970
Using a foot driven wheel, a potter
fashions a large water jug from
local clay. In the background,
several young girls watch from a
respectable distance.

CHILLUM SELLER
KANDAHAR, 1973
Most of the clay containers shown are water jugs, or *kozas*, used to serve water. The long-necked containers, known as *sorai*, are used to collect water. The objects in the upper left and right with the wide mouths are *zerbaghali,* used to create a kind of musical drum by tightly stretching an animal skin across the mouth.

CROWDED BUS
NEAR JALALABAD, 1971
Sometimes the miracle of the Afghan
serwes, or bus service, is two-fold:
the number of individuals who can
actually clamber aboard a bus and the
fact that the busses are kept
running at all. Here, a smiling load of
travelers heads north out of Jalalabad.

RIDING HOME LATE, WINTER
JALALABAD, 1971
Two men astride their donkeys pass down a rural lane at day's end. The mud walls serve to demarcate property ownership as well as divide various crops. In the background the mountains of Nuristan are illuminated by the setting sun.

RUG WEAVERS WITH THEIR WARES
KABUL, 1975
Newly woven rugs, fresh from looms in the provinces, are displayed on a retaining wall along the Kabul River. The art of weaving is as important today as it was in the 1970s.   During that period, rug merchants' shops brimmed with sought-after examples of both antique and new rugs and an array of other textiles and handicrafts.

SEA OF SHEEP
BADAKHSHAN PROVINCE, 1971
The importance of sheep to the Afghans might not be overstated. A source of food, wool for clothing, carpet weaving and objects of daily use and importance, the fat-rumped Afghan sheep is known as Afghan Arabi. Not to be confused with the Karakul sheep used for their luxurious skins, this pendulous-eared variety is known for its ability to adapt to the harsh environment, frequent drought conditions and high elevations of Afghanistan.

SHOPPING FOR POTS AND PANS
KABUL BAZAAR, 1973
A man shops for cooking pots in the
Kabul bazaar. Bazaars are often
organized so that similar items - alu-
minum pots, pottery, shoes, cloth, plas-
tic wares, for example - are all grouped
together in the marketplace. Known as
dokan, they seem to simplify the shopping process and regulate the pricing
as a result. Foreign shoppers quickly
learn the art of bargaining.

THE KITE FLYER
KABUL, 1975
Ignoring the dangers of flying his kite from the elevated roof-top, a *batcha* or Afghan boy deftly controls his kite as a horse-drawn carriage, known as a *gaudi*, passes below. The gaudi serves the ever-present need of providing short distance transport. In this case, a *burkha*-clad mother and her daughter are its passengers.

VILLAGE TAILOR
BADAKSHAN PROVINCE, 1971
A wizened elder tailor, or *khayat*,
applies the final stitches to a multi-
zipper pocketed *waskat*. This versatile
vest is worn by most Afghan men.

MAN IN *PAKOL* HAT
ON THE ROAD IN BADAKHSHAN
PROVINCE, 1971
A well-dressed, well-groomed man wears
a pakol hat made of fine woolen felt. The
hat is common amongst the men of the
region of the Afghan provinces of Nuristan
and Konar. Some scholars and writers
have linked the local appearance of the
pakol to the invasions of Alexander the
Great in the 4th century B.C. Regardless
of its origin, it is now distinctly Afghan and
quite popular.

POTTER'S FAMILY
BAMIAN, 1970
Several members of a village family gather among a collection of water jugs and trays made in the town of Bamian. Numerous caves are seen in the background along with beautifully constructed stone dwellings.

ROCK PILES, TRUCK, MEN AND DONKEYS
BADAKHSHAN PROVINCE, 1971
On the banks of the *Darya-i-Kowkche*, or Kowkche River, men on donkeys pass by large, neatly arranged piles of river rock destined to be used for building construction.

TWO DONKEYS WORKING
FEYDZABAD, 1971
Donkeys are ever-present beasts of burden in Afghanistan. Here on the main street of Feydzabad, they bear the weight of building timbers, sharing the road with heavy, highly decorated lorries, busy pedestrians and curious children. Merchant stalls along the way offer a variety of goods for sale.

AFGHAN SUNSET
NEAR JALALABAD, 1971

The list below will assist the viewer in locating the cities, towns, villages and provinces where the photos were taken.

(1) BADAKHSHAN PROVINCE, city of Feydzabad and surrounding area: pages 11, 20, 32, 33, 49, 52, 53, 56 and back cover

(2) BAMIAN PROVINCE and village: pages 28, 29, 44, 54 and front cover

(3) GHAZNI PROVINCE and city: page 30

(4) KANDAHAR PROVINCE and city: pages 12, 22, 26, 34, 37, 38, 45

(5) KABAL PROVINCE and city: pages 8, 9, 15, 17, 18, 21, 23, 24, 25, 27, 31, 35, 40, 41, 42, 43, 48, 50, 51, 58

(6) NANGARHAR PROVINCE, city of Jalalabad and Khyber Pass: pages 10, 13, 14, 19, 46, 47, 57, 61

(7) NIMRUZ PROVINCE, village of Lash-i-Jouayn: page 36

(8) PARVAN PROVINCE, near the town of Charikar: page 16

KABUL, 1970
The photographer tries his hand at kite fighting

Over several years in the early 1970s, I had the good fortune to photograph in Afghanistan. This was a special time few Americans witnessed; it was before the Soviet occupation and the ensuing civil war and subsequent rise of the Taliban. I fell in love with the Afghan people, their art and culture, their families and their history. I grew to admire their goodness, generosity and their fierce independence.

In 1970 Afghanistan was about as remote a place as any on earth. Tucked away in the north east corner of Central Asia, it was however on the "Silk Road" of the time. This was the track that Hippies followed to get to India, Nepal and beyond. I had known little about Afghanistan until one night around a camp-fire on the beach near the town of Vai, at the very eastern tip of Crete. There I met a young woman from New Zealand who had just crossed Asia by bus. She had the most remarkable tales to tell about the mountainous desert kingdom: sleeping in the *chai-khana*, tea houses, riding on the tops of reeling rickety buses through perilous gorges, 150 foot Buddhas carved into cliffs, exploring ancient caravansaray. I knew I had to go.

I first arrived in Afghanistan in the summer of 1970. It was near the end of August and it was hot. I entered through the border crossing at Spin Boldak/Chaman, from Pakistan, south of Kandahar. I remember looking at the thermometer in the hotel I booked into in Kandahar at the Herat gate. It read 126

degrees. I had hitch-hiked to Kandahar from Istanbul, via Tehran and across Iran's *Dasht-i-Margo* - the Desert of Death. It was nearly, but not quite, as bad as it sounds. Thus began my time in Afghanistan. Over the next five years I visited the country five times and spent nearly 40 months there. I had not planned to stay that long, but illness kept me there through the first winter. Then spring arrived and I ventured into the countryside. The more I saw and experienced the more I was taken by the people, the landscape and culture.

I loved being there. Travel was cheap, safe and easy. The people were friendly, open and generous beyond their means. The sounds, sights and smells of everyday life were exhilarating. The contrasts were amazing; the deserts ran on seemingly without end, the mountains concealed green oases of vineyards, lush gardens and apricot and mulberry groves were everywhere. Even the names of the mountains were intoxicating: the Koh-I Baba, the Hindu Kush, the Pamirs, This was indeed a different world. It seemed I could not leave.

I personally developed and printed these images during that period and kept them for my own use, showing them to friends and family as a record of my travels. For many years it had been my intention to revisit the photos, edit them and relearn the printing process in order to share the images on a broader scale. In 2004, I had the opportunity to do so and began the process.

Regrettably, 30 years of casual storage in the south Florida heat and humidity had resulted in some damage to the film, thus the negatives needed to be scanned and restored digitally to remove spots and distortions. Reproducing the images photographically proved problematic so I have presented the exhibition series as inkjet prints using archival inks and state-of-the-art fiber-based paper.

Photographs are a deft combination of time and place, light, composition, texture and content. In many of these images the sense of timelessness is strong, with little or no evidence of modern intrusion. I found the Afghans easily approachable, camera in hand, but discovered that concealing the camera beneath my jacket meant I would not gather a crowd of youngsters following me, clamoring for *bakshish* - a little gift, and for their pictures to be taken. It is often noted that very few of the photos include girls or women. This is indeed so; even in the more relaxed and enlightened time of my visit, I felt it somehow intrusive to photograph women. I felt awkward and I regret this now.

All images were originally produced using a variety of 35mm Kodak, Ilford and Agfa films. All photos were shot using Nikon F and Nikkormat cameras and Nikon 24mm, 28mm, 50mm and 105mm lenses.

Joseph Hoyt
2008

NEAR JALALABAD
SPRING. 1971
The cow skins, or *poste-a-gow*, being carried to the river.

NEAR JALALABAD
SPRING. 1971
Floating the Kabul River on inflated cow skins with three unidentified Afghans. The presence of the tennis racquet remains a mystery.
Photo by Gary Crandall

ACKNOWLEDGEMENTS

Special thanks are due to numerous individuals without whose help and guidance this book and the accompanying exhibition would not have been possible:

My wife Nancy Meyer, who kept after me for 25 years to revisit the photos.

My son Adam J. Hoyt, who had an eye for reviewing the images and endured the stories that accompany each.

My brother Seth Hoyt, for his editing expertise and great ideas.

Margot Ammidown, who accompanied me to Afghanistan in 1974 and who provides encouragement still.

Mario Algaze for his critical eye and encouragement.

Clyde Butcher, who took an interest from the start and provided many hours of his time and the benefit of years of experience in selecting and printing images.

Michael L. Carlebach for his scholar's perspective and kind support.

Willy Kasuli, fellow traveler, advisor, supporter, friend.

Nazifa Najem Given and Dr. Reza Najem who helped in creating meaningful captions to the photos.

Mr. Khalid Ziai of Limoges, France, director of the website www.afghanistan-photos.com for his help in translation and for recommending my photos to visitors to his website.

Mr. Hamid Elmi, former Cultural Attaché, Embassy of Afghanistan, Washington, DC for his correspondence, support and the gift of a fine pakol hat.

Hope Herman Wurmfeld who, in 1969, encouraged me to actually use my camera.

Lisa Vestal, Chief Curator, and the staff of the San Francisco Public Library.

Many others provided assistance and encouragement in countless ways. They deserve recognition and thanks:

Bhakti Baxter	Carroll Fisher	Barbara Parker
Junius Beebe	Tom Graboski	Christine Rupp
Gendry Bolsano	Mark Gaggia	Raymond Santiago
Maria O'Meara Bransfield	Mitchell Kaplan	Annette and Alberto
Nikki Butcher	MaryMar Keenan	Delgado Stenner
Bo Carper	David Kenner	Matt Stock
Gary Crandall	David Lukas	Kim Usiak
Denise Delgado	Cristina Nosti	Peter A. Zorn, Jr.
Lisa Dority	Stephen L. Meeks